THE ME TOO MOVEMENT

MEN'S GUIDE ON HOW TO BEHAVE WITH WOMEN

By Alice Jones

Dedication

To all the women in the world who feel disrespected, unappreciated, harrassed and meant to feel less than.   To all the men who want to learn how to be more compassionate, respectful and kind to the women in their lives.

Introduction

In the days of the ME TOO movement, I felt the need to help men better understand why women are angry and fed up. I hope to offer some suggestions for men who wish to learn how to respect women. We don't want to take over the world (yet), we just wan't to be treated as equals.

I've had my share of sexual assault, harrassment, lude comments and more over the years in my professional and personal life. My attitude about sex has been effected by those experiences as well as my personal opinions about the male race.

We've seen powerful men lose their jobs and reputations under allegations of sexual misconduct. We've seen women marching in the streets telling men we've had enough. We've seen numerous women tell their stories of rape, assault, verbal abuse, sexual touching and more. One thing is clear, it is time for men to sit up and take notice. Women have had enough of being less than and we demand equal respect.

I hope this guidebook will offer some insight on what is appropriate and inappropriate behavior. It also includes some suggestions to change the mindset of how men should treat women. I encourage all men to teach others and call out bad behavior when they see it.

CHAPTER ONE - OUR CULTURE

We cannot deny the fact that there is a problem with some men in the United States and the way they behave towards women. I'm not throwing all men into this category but the recent public knowledge should be a wake up call. After our President boasted about sexual harrassment and has numerous women accusing him of sexual assault, I sighed. We all know his past don't we? After the Olympics doctor, Larry Nasser was accused of abusing over 100 of our Olympic girls over a twenty year period, I cried. As these girls faced him in court and told their stories I cried. As more stories were revealed about Hollywood Moguls and other powerful people assaulting women I was mad.

Women's Experiences

Times have changed from the 1940's,

1950's when men controlled the household, the money, the decisions. Women were stay at home moms who raised the kids, did all the cleaning and cooking. Women can work now and be independent, earn their own money and choose whether or not to marry and have kids. We don't NEED men anymore for protection or financial support.

My own experience includes being molested by a stranger at age 10 which was traumatic and seriously effected me. The next experience was age 14 when I was at summer camp. I woke in my little camp cabin in the middle of the night to find a camp counselor laying all over me and wanting to have sex. When I was in high school and college I experienced all the cat calls, rude comments and so much more. In college, I was harrased on two jobs by the owner and experienced more of it being a waitress for many years during college.

I remember when I was a teenager I dressed down and covered up so I might receive less harrasment. I was so shy, scared and didn't want to stand out in any way. Sometimes I wished I could have worn tighter jeans or an attractive top, but I did not. I did not want the unsolicited comments that would come from boys and men. All through my professional years I experienced ongoing harrasment. One of my boyfriends raped me after a serious injury since I was totally helpless to fight him off. I was breaking up with him and his response was violent and psychotic. As an adult I also experienced extensive emotional and verbal abuse in my second marriage. I was told I was worthless, stupid and that I could never get along without him. That was the shortest marriage in history and I got out quickly.

This is also the reason I choose to be self employed for the last 25 years because I was tired of constantly dealing with bosses who used their power over my job and paycheck to their advantage.   Many women deal with this harrasment in the workplace and we want it to stop.

I think the most hurtful part of being a women and experiences these awful things is that many times no one believes our story.   The real hurt comes from not being believed.   How dare they say we misinterpreted?   How dare they say we are liars? Do men call out other men for being liars?   Why is it always assumed that women can't be believed?

Media and Video Games

Let's face it we all know that TV, movies, video games and advertising are filled with images of beautiful sexy women to sell products and entice the male audience. Some video games in particular show violent scenes of women being abused and raped.

Why is our culture allowing this to continue?

One great example of this in terms of media is the Fox News company that has recently been exposed for it continued culture of sexual harrassment in the workplace.   Women were required to wear short skirts and sexy tops as part of their job description.   Men on the air would talk dirty about them while they were sitting next to them.   They would make jokes or comments about women all the time.   This is not a culture that women want any part of.   How would the men feel if the women on air commented on their small private parts?   How would these men feel if their daughters, mothers or sisters were talked about this way?

STATISTICS

In the United States, sexual assault occurs every 98 seconds.

According to the Rainn.org statistics site since 1998 there have been over 18 million women have been raped.   The most vulenrable ages are 12 to 34 years old. This means one out of six women in America will be raped or assaulted in their lifetime. Three percent of men or 2 million men were also raped since 1998.   Seven in ten rapes are committed by someone the victim knows.

In the workplace over 33 million women have been harrassed by bosses and co-workers.

In another study they found 75% of women who reported the workplace harrassment got demoted or fired or have their reputation slandered.

LAWS

I've long been frustrated with laws surrounding sexual assault, rape, and the other laws that discriminate against women. I never understood why there would be a time limit on accusing someone of rape? There should never be a statute of limitation on sexual assault. It is a violent crime that causes life long trauma. I hope someday the law will be changed on a federal level (that states cannot change) removing any time limitation on accusations of sexual assault.

In addition to the time limitations is the insult of light sentences and no accountability. Statistically over 99 percent of men will walk free without any consequences. Is this fair? No. Women deserve justice too.

In these law suits, women's morality, sexual partners, appearance are all used against them to discredit their stories.   Most rape victims have to pay to have a rape kit done which costs from $400 and up to $1500.

I've also watched over the years the constant reversal of laws that women have worked so hard to achieve.   Birth control, abortion rights and many others.   In fact I often wondered how men would feel if they banned Viagra or condoms?   Would men be willing to have random sex without condoms and be financially responsible for every child they father?   If men and women didn't have some form of birth control the population would explode and we would not survive due to limited resources.

Many states still have in place an outrageous law that allows the rapists to have parental rights of any children born out of rape.   The mothers have to see, interact with and share custody of their children with their rapist.   I saw a TV special about this issue and was horrified. Who thinks this is okay?   It is NOT.   The females have already been assaulted and have to deal with the rape forever.   Why aren't their rapists in prison?   What gives them any rights to children who came out of a violent act?   One mother expressed deep concern about her little daughter spending time with her mother's rapist. How can she make sure her daughter is protected and not raped by this man? These laws clearly must be changed and part of that change is making sure that rapists are in prison for their crimes, not allowed to parent.

CHAPTER TWO

Men's Experiences

In light of this ME TOO movement, I've heard men say women are over reacting, taking it too far, lying about their allegations and other insulting comments. I've also heard men of integrity say they are getting backlash for speaking out FOR women.   Some are afraid to speak up for fear of consequences. They have also talked about feeling like they have to walk on eggshells around women. Some companies are now afraid to hire women for fear of law suits. I've heard men say they felt shame that maybe they said something wrong or offended someone.   Some say it's just men being men, locker room talk, the way guys are with each other sometimes. Other men say they do these things to make themselves feel better or to be able to brag to their friends about it.   It does seem to come from an insecurity they feel within themselves.   There is an easy solution to this – don't say or do things that are offensive and there are no worries. You don't have to be afraid of us – just do the right thing !

We know that many young boys are taught from childhood to be a man.   Be assertive, confident, powerful.   Generations before us were taught sometimes that they were superior to women.   They were smarter, faster, in charge of the family, the sole decision maker and the worker of the family.   Generations before us expected women to stay home and raise the family and take care of the house.   Women had very little opportunity to work.   We know that many boys from generations past turned into grown men who held the same beliefs.

Times are different now and men's behavior needs to change with the times.

I encourage men to go beyond the "expected" roles and open up to the fact that women are powerful, smart and important.   Women have choices now and men need to adjust to the new reality of equal treatment.

CHAPTER THREE -

Guidelines and Rules to Follow

* Don't whistle or comment when we are walking by

* When speaking to us, look us in the eye not the breast or butt

* Treat us like equals - same pay, same opportunities

* Treat women like you would your mother, sister, daughter, granddaughter

* Quit interrupting us when we are talking. What we have to say is just as important as what you say.

* Quit calling us hysterical, bitches, too emotional when we get angry, hurt or loud. We are entitled to our own feelings too.

* If you are married and wanting an

affair, how about get a divorce first?   If you want to have an affair are you also okay with your wife having an affair?   I see so many internet ads of men looking for affairs and submissive women to fulfill their needs.   The number of these kind of ads is disturbing.   Why men think women would be attracted to this idea is even more perplexing.

*   We are not your baby's, honey's, darling's or sweethearts.   Those names are intimate and personal and we do not appreciate it.   STOP SAYING IT.   The only people who allowed to call us that are our parents and our lovers.   For example, if I had a husband who walked around calling other women honey then it would mean nothing if he said it to me.   How would men feel if your wife went around calling all men darling and honey?   My response to men is usually "My name is Alice and I'm not your baby."   Perhaps we

should make up names for men. It is not cute, sweet or normal so quit doing it!

* If you choose to pay for a dinner or lunch out that DOES NOT mean you automatically get sex. Men are sometimes upset when women insist on paying their own bill or their share of the check.   The wonder why....it's pretty obvious.   You don't get sex for paying for dinner and the assumption that you would is insulting. What if we offered to pay for your dinner and expected you to come do chores or build a deck or clean our garage? Wouldn't you laugh at that?

*   You are NOT allowed to touch us anywhere without CONSENT.   If a women is intoxicated she cannot give CONSENT which means you better leave her alone.   If a woman says NO and you don't stop it is a criminal offense and can be on your record for life.

* Quit making assumptions about what women wear. We are allowed to look good without being harrassed. We are not dressing nicely for men - we are doing it for ourselves. Just because a woman may look sexy isn't an open invitation for men to be rude.

* We are not your mothers or housekeepers and men need to learn how to do laundry, cook, clean and do half the chores.

* Quit being offended when we say no to sex. It's usually about being tired or stressed and has nothing personal to do with you. If you want your wife less stressed than help out more. Help complete the chores, get the kids to bed so there is less exhaustion and stress. Women appreciate this.

* If you feel you have no control over your behavior please get counseling.

THINGS TO DO THAT WILL HELP

Small things count more than big things.

*   Say thank you to your spouse or girlfriend, mother, daugher. Be grateful and show it.

*   Do nice little things - sticky notes on the mirror, nice card or letter   I remember when I was married to my first husband and we were struggling with money and couldn't afford nice gifts for each other.   The greatest Valentine's gift I ever received from him was a wooden heart painted with a little poem on it.   He made it by hand in the basement in secret and worked hard on it.   It meant so much to me because he took the time, he cared enough to show he loved me.   In other years we would sometimes write each other letters and I cherished those.   Reminder: the littlest things make the most difference.

* Pitch in - it's your house and family too so split the chores, work like a team

* A compliment or kind word goes a long way

* Cook dinner for her sometimes   - it can be simple or fancy but the time and effort you took to do it will mean more than any food you cook.

* Remember birthdays and anniversaries. You have no excuse to forget now because you can set those on your phone and reminders to yourself a week before the event.

*   Take the kids out for the day or watch them for a weekend.   She needs alone time, friend time and her own time without the family.

CHAPTER FOUR = Share the Rules & Teach Your Kids

One of the reasons I am writing this guide is for men to do better. For men with integrity to start speaking up and speaking out. You know which of your friends, family or co-workers say crude things about women. Ask them to stop. Remind them that they wouldn't want men talking about their sisters, daughters or mothers that way.   Please help teach other men to be more respectful. Call out bad behavior when you see or hear it. You can't just stay silent anymore.   All women will appreciate this.

Teaching others to act better starts with childhood. For those of you who are parents please teach your kids to be respectful of others. Please show by example what it looks like when a couple is kind to each other, works as a team, respects each other. Teach your boys and girls to be kind to all human beings. Teach your boys to respect girls and women. There is hope that new generations will understand the importance of this issue and change the culture of men against women.

Questions To Consider

Why can't women walk down the street freely without comments or whistles?

Why can't women go to a bar for a drink without every man assuming she is there to find a man?

What would men do if women refused to have sex with them forever (including prostitutes)?

What would men do if women refused to cook and clean for them (no paid housekeepers allowed)?

What would men do if they could never have children because no one would have sex with them?

How would men feel if they were raped or assaulted by another man?   Would they want justice?   Would they be hurt if they weren't believed?

Do men realize they wouldn't even exist or be on earth without a women giving birth to them?

CONCLUSION

Keep in mind these are my opinions, experiences, thoughts and I don't claim to speak for others.   However in my lifetime I have many of the same things from other women.

I just hope that men will step up and stand up for us.   There's so much you can do as men that will help this issue.   As women we are sick and tired of being treated as second class.   As men you no doubt have a mother, sister, wife, daughter.   Please keep in mind how you would feel if men treated the women in your life this way. Talk and teach others, teach your kids, call out this behavior in other men.   THANK YOU !

Printed in Great Britain
by Amazon